CENTRAL AFRICAN REPUBLIC
in Pictures

Matt Doeden

WITHDRAWN

Twenty-First Century Books

Contents

Lerner Publishing Group, Inc., realizes that current information and statistics quickly become out of date. To extend the usefulness of the Visual Geography Series, we developed www.vgsbooks.com, a website offering links to up-to-date information, as well as in-depth material, on a wide variety of subjects. All the websites listed on www.vgsbooks.com have been carefully selected by researchers at Lerner Publishing Group, Inc. However, Lerner Publishing Group, Inc., is not responsible for the accuracy or suitability of the material on any website other than www.lernerbooks.com. It is recommended that students using the Internet be supervised by a parent or teacher. Links on www.vgsbooks.com will be regularly reviewed and updated as needed.

Website address: www.lernerbooks.c◼

Twenty-First Century Books
A division of Lerner Publishing Group, Inc.
241 First Avenue North
Minneapolis, MN 55401 U.S.A.

web enhanced @ www.vgsbooks.com

CULTURAL LIFE   46

▶ Folktales and Literature. Religion. Art. Music and
  Dance. Media. Holidays and Celebrations. Sports.
  Food.

THE ECONOMY   56

▶ Agriculture, Forestry, and Fishing. Services.
  Industry and Mining. Foreign Trade.
  Transportation and Communication. The Future.

FOR MORE INFORMATION

Library of Congress Cataloging-in-Publication Data

Doeden, Matt.
    Central African Republic in pictures / by Matt Doeden.
       p.   cm. — (Visual geography series)
    Includes bibliographical references and index.
    ISBN 978-1-57505-952-5 (lib. bdg. : alk. paper)
    1. Central African Republic—Pictorial works—Juvenile literature. 2. Central African Republic—Juvenile
literature. I. Title.
DT546.324.D64 2009
967.41—dc22   2008014331

Manufactured in the United States of America
1 2 3 4 5 6 - BP - 14 13 12 11 10 09

INTRODUCTION

One of the world's poorest countries, the Central African Republic (CAR) lies at the very heart of Africa. This landlocked nation is a land of contrast. It stretches from the edge of a desert in the north, across open grasslands, and into Africa's rich rain forest. Its people, likewise, are full of contrast. As many as eighty ethnic groups call the nation home. While most of the population is rural, the capital city of Bangui is booming.

The history of the CAR's people is long. With no written record, little is known of the region's earliest peoples. Great stone monuments hint at an advanced civilization more than twenty-five hundred years ago, but details about the people who built them have been lost to time. The written historical record is largely blank until Arab slave raiders entered the region beginning in the seventeenth century. That contact marks the beginning of a tragic time for Africans, with foreign powers and local peoples capturing and selling off local inhabitants to slave traders. To escape the slave traders, many Africans moved from

place to place, avoiding contact with other peoples. The historic isolation among groups has contributed to the difficulty Central Africans have had in developing a modern national identity.

France gained control of the region in the late 1800s, naming its new colony Oubangui-Chari. European companies leased large tracts of land from the French colonial government. This arrangement changed the region's agricultural focus from small, food-growing farms to large cotton, coffee, and tobacco plantations. Although the economy developed, the profits belonged to European investors. Central Africans remained poorly fed and inadequately housed, which increased the resentment against the colonial government.

Since gaining independence in 1960, the CAR has maintained close links with France. France provides the nation with significant amounts of financial aid each year, and French investors make up most of the CAR's meager foreign investment. French remains one of the nation's official languages, although only a small percentage of the

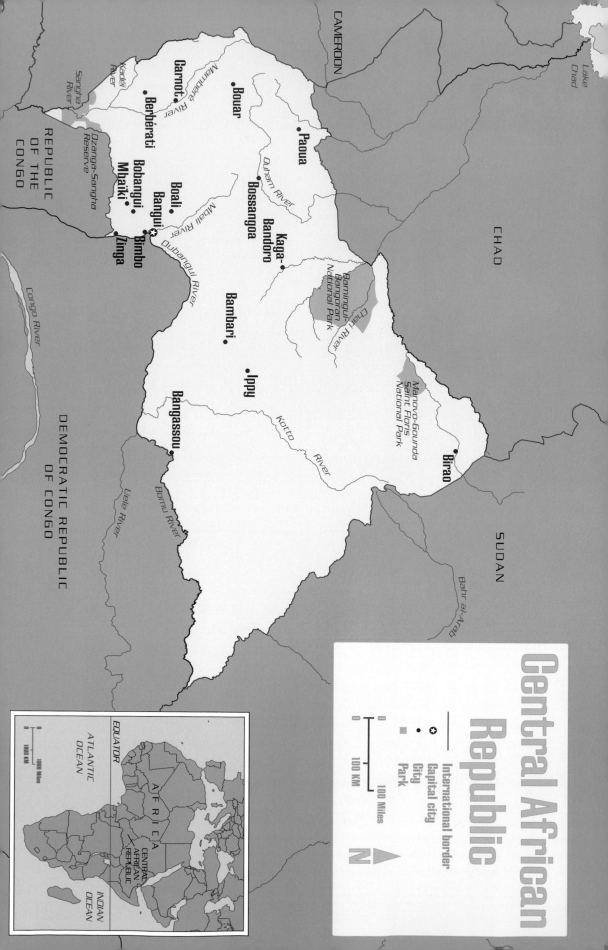

population speaks it. Since 1960 the nation has faltered under inefficient and often corrupt leadership. The level of production achieved by some parts of the economy in the early years of independence has been lost. Despite many promises of political freedom for Central Africans, government officials have abused their power. National leaders have postponed elections, broken their country's laws, and taken financial advantage of their governmental positions.

The Central African Republic faces a host of challenges in the present and near future. The nation's economy is in shambles. The government doesn't have enough money to pay its employees. Constant rebellions and attempts to take over the government have badly destabilized the nation, and political unrest in the neighboring countries of Chad and Sudan has spilled across CAR borders. Short life expectancy, low literacy rates, and an undeveloped infrastructure intensify the challenges.

But hope remains. The nation is rich in natural resources, from diamonds to timber to natural beauty. A strong leader and stable government would be important first steps toward progress and prosperity.

THE LAND

The Central African Republic lies near the middle of the African continent. It shares borders on the west with Cameroon, on the north with Chad, on the east with Sudan, on the south with the Democratic Republic of Congo (DRC), and on the southwest with the Republic of the Congo. Completely landlocked, the CAR is more than 375 miles (600 kilometers) from the nearest sea—the Gulf of Guinea on the Atlantic Ocean. With 240,535 square miles (622,984 sq. km) of territory, the CAR is slightly smaller than the U.S. state of Texas.

▷ Topography

The large Plateau region, which is broken up by many rivers, covers most of the CAR. This area of generally flat land stretches across the middle of the nation, with most of it having an elevation of 2,000 to 3,000 feet (610 to 914 meters) above sea level. Only isolated *kaga* (granite peaks), occasional ridges, and river valleys break up the otherwise flat expanse of the Plateau. Acting as a dividing point for the country's river systems, the Plateau directs northern waterways into the Lake Chad basin and southern rivers into the Congo River basin. The southwestern part of the Plateau includes diamond-rich formations of sandstone.

In the west, the Plateau rises into the Yadé Massif. This granite highland straddles the border with Cameroon and Chad. It is composed of kaga that vary greatly in height. The region includes the Karre Mountains. This small range boasts the nation's highest peak, Mount Ngaoui, which rises to a height of 4,658 feet (1,420 m.) above sea level.

In the east, the Bongo Massif and the smaller Tondou Massif rise along the nation's border with Sudan. Several peaks in this highland region stand more than 4,000 feet (1,219 m), with the tallest, Mount Toussoro, reaching a height of 4,364 feet (1,330 m). The source of the Bahr al-Arab (River of the Arabs) is found within this region.

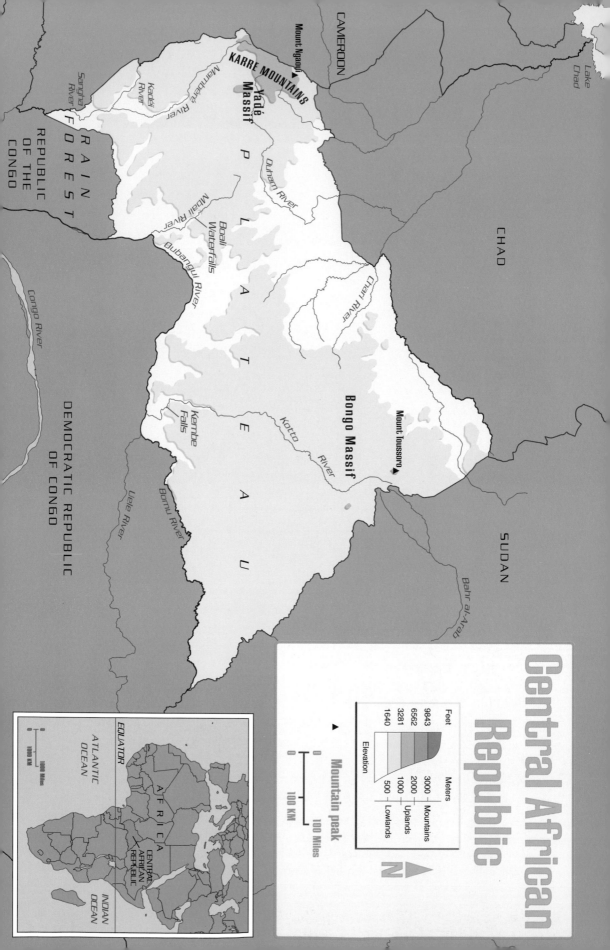

Central African Republic

CAMEROON

Lake
Chad

Mount Ngaoui ▲
KARRE MOUNTAINS
Yadé
Massif

Kadéi
River

Mambéré River

Sangha River

REPUBLIC
OF THE
CONGO

R A I N   F O R E S T

Mbali River

Ouham River

Baali
Waterfalls

Oubangui River

P L A T E A U

CHAD

Chari River

Bongo Massif

Mount Toussoro ▲

Congo River

DEMOCRATIC REPUBLIC
OF CONGO

Kembe
Falls

Kotto River

Uele River

Bomu River

SUDAN

Bahr al-Arab

Elevation

Feet	Meters	
9843	3000	Mountains
6562	2000	
3281	1000	Uplands
1640	500	Lowlands

▲ Mountain peak

N

Scale:
0 — 100 Miles
0 — 100 KM

EQUATOR

ATLANTIC
OCEAN

A F R I C A

CENTRAL
AFRICAN
REPUBLIC

INDIAN
OCEAN

0 — 1000 Miles
0 — 1000 KM

In the southwest, the lush Rain Forest region runs along the Oubangui River. The CAR's rain forest is the far northern edge of a much larger rain forest that covers much of the west-central part of the continent. In total, it is the second-largest rain forest in the world. Only the Amazon Rain Forest in South America covers more ground.

▷ Rivers

The CAR has a wealth of rivers. Because the nation is landlocked and it has no big lakes, its rivers are the main sources of water for people, animals, and crops. They are also critical for transportation in a country with poorly developed roads and lacking a railroad system.

The region's longest and most navigable river is the Oubangui (also called the Ubangi), which covers 1,400 miles (2,254 km). It stems from the Bomu and the Uele rivers, which begin in the DRC. The Oubangui River flows westward from the town of Bangassou and traces most of the nation's border with the DRC. After passing through Bangui—the Central African Republic's capital—the river abruptly turns south, leaving the CAR and traveling to the Congo basin. The river swells during the rainy season, often carrying three times its usual volume of water.

The Chari (or Shari) River begins in the CAR. The Chari and its many tributaries (smaller joining rivers) flow northward into Chad, and the Chari partly defines the CAR's border with its northern neighbor.

The **Boali waterfalls** on the Mbali River of southwestern CAR are a popular destination for tourists.

The month of May often brings heavy rains to the CAR, especially in the south. Deadly floods often follow, as rivers rise several feet in just a few hours. One such flood occurred in 2005, leaving twenty thousand people homeless.

The Chari winds 590 miles (949 km) before it empties into Lake Chad.

The Sangha River forms part of the Central African Republic's western border with Cameroon. It forms just south of the town of Berbérati, where the Kadéï and Mambéré rivers join. This western river and its tributaries cut a 1,000-mile-long (1,600 km) valley through western Africa. The Sangha eventually empties into the Congo River.

◉ Climate

The Central African Republic lies a little more than 300 miles (483 km) north of the equator (an imaginary line that separates the Northern and Southern hemispheres). But despite this location, the country doesn't register the extreme heat and humidity common to most equatorial regions. Altitude and rainfall help to moderate the temperature, which ranges between 80 and 90°F (27 and 32°C) most of the year, though it can soar as high as 104°F (40°C).

The Central African Republic has three climate zones. The northern part of the country borders on the Sahel, an area between the Sahara and more fertile areas to the south. A hot, dry, dusty wind called the Harmattan blows across this zone. The Harmatten carries dust from the Sahara, often covering everything in a fine red powder. The northern part of the nation has a six-month dry season, which occurs between November and April. During the remainder of the year, this zone has a wet season in which about 30 inches (76 centimeters) of rain may fall.

The large plateau that makes up most of the country receives more rain and has a shorter dry season than the northern zone. As much as 60 inches (152 cm) of rain may fall on the plateau during the wet months. Rainfall is often intense, with several inches coming down in an hour. In this central climate area, temperatures during the dry season sometimes drop to 50°F (10°C) at night.

The southern part of the country has the wettest climate, and the dry season is only a couple of months long. Some areas have no dry season at all. This climate zone sees about 70 inches (178 cm) of rain each year. The heaviest downpours often lead to heavy flooding.

◉ Flora and Fauna

Each climate zone supports vegetation suited to its rainfall level, temperature, and soil. In the arid northern region that borders the Sahel,

A **giraffe** looks over the landscape in the Dzanga-Sangha Reserve in southwestern CAR.

few varieties of plants can survive. Acacia trees produce gum arabic (a sticky material used in making candy and medicine). Shea trees also grow in this area. Their seeds produce an oil called shea butter, which is used in food, soap, lotions, and candles. Shrubs and tough grasses also thrive in the north.

Savanna—a region of grasses and trees—covers the central plateau. The variety of plants that grow on the savanna depends on the amount of moisture the region receives and the number of grazing animals it supports. Human inhabitants have altered the landscape by clearing it for farming.

The thick rain forest along the Oubangui River covers portions of the southwestern corner of the country. The upper branches of trees as tall as 150 feet (46 m) make a leafy canopy that shades the shrubs and mosses growing at the lower levels of the forest. Many useful trees thrive in the area, including sapele, mahogany, iroko, and obeche. Strong liana vines climb many of the tree trunks.

Giraffes, antelope, African buffalo, rhinos, hippos, and elephants roam the northern and central regions of the Central African Republic,

The CAR's wild elephants are in grave danger of dying out. Despite laws to protect the herds, widespread poaching of elephants for their valuable ivory tusks threatens to wipe out the great beasts.

especially in Bamingui-Bangoran National Park. Predatory animals such as lions, leopards, and cheetahs hunt zebra, antelopes, and other prey on the savanna and in the forests. In the south, chimpanzees, gorillas, monkeys, bongos (forest antelope), and forest elephants call the lush rain forests home. Crocodiles swim alongside a wide variety of fish in the nation's many rivers.

BUSHMEAT

The hunting of wild animals, or bushmeat, is a growing problem in Africa, as people kill more animals than natural breeding cycles can replace. The result is what some scientists call the empty forest syndrome, where a healthy-looking forest is actually devoid of animal wildlife.

The term *bushmeat* often refers specifically to the great apes, including gorillas *(above)* and chimpanzees. Hunters slaughter large adult apes for food. They sell off smaller, younger apes as pets. The practice has a devastating effect on wild ape populations.

▷ Natural Resources

The CAR is a poor and undeveloped country. But it does boast some valuable natural resources. Its mineral resources—most notably diamonds—are among its largest exports. The nation's diamonds lie mainly in the sandstone deposits found in the western part of the country. These precious stones have accounted for as much as half of the nation's exports. Other mineral resources in the CAR include gold, copper, iron, and uranium (used as a fuel in nuclear reactors). Many experts believe the nation may also have untapped oil reserves in the northern part of the country, but if that is the case, they remain undiscovered. Hydroelectric dams on the CAR's many rivers produce power for turbine engines that make electricity, another valuable resource.

The forests of the south provide another valuable resource—timber. Logging is a rapidly growing business in the nation, with production more than doubling since the early 1990s.

Environmental Challenges

While logging is an economic boon, it is an environmental disaster. Logging companies do not replace the trees they cut down, resulting in a dramatic reduction of forested land. Forest wildlife is forced into smaller and smaller areas. Slash-and-burn agriculture also contributes to the loss of forest. Farmers cut and burn sections of forest so they can use the land for farming. A similar problem arises with the intense mining of the country's lands. Mining companies often leave behind barren, scarred land that is useless to people and wildlife alike.

Loggers take down trees near Mbaïki. **Logging** is both a growing economic boon and an environmental threat in the CAR.

Visit www.vgsbooks.com for links to websites with additional information about the natural resources and environmental challenges that face the Central African Republic.

The CAR's wildlife faces other threats related to human activity. Herders graze their animals on lands set aside for wildlife, driving animals into still smaller areas. People poach (illegally hunt) animals such as elephants, giraffes, and gorillas to sell on the black market (ivory from elephant tusks is especially valuable). Even animals in protected areas, such as the Manovo-Gounda Saint Floris National Park, may be in danger. The nation doesn't have the resources to enforce laws to protect wildlife, however.

A process called desertification threatens the far northeast part of the country. Year by year, the Sahara and the Sahel slowly expand, taking up more and more territory. Plant and animal life struggle to survive on the increasingly arid (dry) land left by this process.

Cities

The CAR is a sparsely populated country, with only one large city. Only 38 percent of its population lives in urban areas. Its average of 18 people per square mile (7 people per sq. km) ranks among the lowest population densities in the center of Africa.

BANGUI (population 622,771) is the nation's capital, largest city, and only real urban area. Established by the French in 1889, the city lies on the banks of the Oubangui River. The city's old section features wide, tree-shaded boulevards and a central market area, both of which reflect its colonial heritage. Most Central Africans in Bangui live in *kodros*—residential neighborhoods whose buildings are made of mud bricks with thatched roofs. Many of these homes lack modern conveniences such as running water, electricity, and sanitation services. The city is the frequent site of political power struggles—often violent—making it one of the most dangerous cities in the world. This problem was highlighted in 1996, when soldiers in the CAR's army rose up against the government because their salaries had not been paid. When the fighting and looting were over, much of Bangui lay in ruins and many people had been killed.

Bangui is home to the Boganda Museum, founded in 1964. The museum offers visitors a wealth of Central African history and culture. It has an exhibit of local (or, indigenous) artifacts, a wide variety of musical instruments, ancient weapons, religious objects, and much more.

OTHER CITIES in the CAR are much smaller. Populations vary widely from season to season as residents return to the countryside for long periods of time to farm or hunt. Bimbo (population 124,176) is the

Bossangoa is a typical small city in the CAR. This photograph shows the main street through the city.

nation's second-largest city. It lies just a few miles south of Bangui along the Oubangui River. Berbérati (population 76,918) is near the Cameroon border. Its proximity to the Dzanga-Sangha Reserve makes it a popular stop among tourists to the country. Other small cities in the CAR include Carnot (population 45,421) in the west; Bambari (population 41,356) in the south central region; Bouar (population 40,353), which lies along the road that leads from Bangui to Cameroon; and Bossangoa (population 36,478) in the northwest. Bossangoa, which lies along the Ouham River (a tributary of the Chari), is famous for its rebellion against French colonial authorities in the early 1900s.

Many Central Africans live in small villages of fewer than one hundred people. More than six thousand of these settlements dot the countryside. Most of the villages are located in the southwest along the Oubangui River or in the northwestern highland area.

A set of great granite stones, called megaliths, set into the earth stands near the city of Bouar. The stones are more than twenty-five hundred years old. Ancient people probably used them to track the movements of the planets and stars.

HISTORY AND GOVERNMENT

Little is known about the early history of the area that makes up the present-day Central African Republic. The ancestors of the Aka (pygmy) people may have lived in the region as early as fifty thousand years ago. These nomadic hunter-gatherers lived off the resources of the forest, hunting for prey and gathering wild plants for food.

Other groups inhabited the area as early as eight thousand years ago. Stone tools that date from about 6000 B.C. indicate that the early populations were also nomadic hunter-gatherers. They moved about the African landscape in search of food and prey. Groups probably competed fiercely for the land's few resources, severely limiting population growth in the region.

Over the centuries, agriculture began to replace the hunter-gatherer lifestyle. By about 1000 B.C., the inhabitants had cleared sections of the thick, dry forest that covered most of the middle of the CAR. They planted grains such as millet and sorghum on small plots of land. As they cut down forest, the characteristics of the savanna that stretches across the modern Central African plateau began to change the landscape.

A more organized civilization began to take shape around 1000 B.C. and thrived for about two thousand years. In about 500 B.C., local farming people in the western portion of the country, near present-day Bouar, carefully arranged megaliths weighing several tons each. The cooperation needed to make and to position these stone monuments reveals that the people who placed the stones were well organized and must have had a degree of social unity. The placement of the stones, which line up with the movements of the planets and stars, also suggests knowledge of astronomy. Scholars know little else, however, about the people of this time or why the civilization went into decline around A.D. 1000.

A Region of Isolation

By around A.D. 1000, several isolated groups were living in the area that would become the CAR. People speaking Adamawan languages had migrated from the west, while Central Sudanic people settled near the

Oubangui River. Meanwhile, small populations of Bantu-speaking people came from west central Africa. For the most part, these groups had little contact with one another.

By this time, farmers were regularly using the slash-and-burn method to clear land for planting. Drought often destroyed crops. Tsetse flies infected animals with deadly diseases, making livestock difficult to raise. Scarcity of food caused conflict among groups as they competed for better farmland and for greater access to game animals.

During the fifteenth and sixteenth centuries, Portuguese and Arab traders wrote accounts of African life, customs, and geography. The reports, many of them considered legendary by modern historians, give little concrete information of these settlements beyond their names— Goaga, Anzica, and Aloa. Parts of the region also fell under the sway of African empires such as Kanem-Borno, Bagirmi, and Darfur. But for the most part, the region that would become the CAR was cut off from the rest of the world.

◉ The Slave Trade Develops

For most of its history, the region of the present-day CAR was not directly connected to any of the main commercial routes that extended through Africa, Europe, and Asia. Outsiders knew virtually nothing about the area. That changed around the seventeenth century. Arab traders ventured farther into middle Africa, bringing with them their culture and religion of Islam. This contact brought trade and new ideas to people who had long been isolated. But the contact also introduced the slave trade.

Although Africans had occasionally been taken from the region as slaves before the first century A.D., the slave trade became central to the economy from the seventeenth to the middle of the nineteenth century. Arab and African traders captured people, ripping them from their homes and families, and sent them as slaves to northern Africa or to the Atlantic coast. From these points, slave ships transported the captives to the Americas or to Middle Eastern markets.

The slave trade brought the region into contact with major African trade routes. In the east, new commercial trade markets developed. Some Arab traders came into the area in the early eighteenth century to exchange their tea, sugar, cloth, salt, and perfume for the ivory that the local people harvested from elephants. The Arab traders also brought seeds and cuttings for new crops, such as maize (corn) and cassava (a root crop)—both of which grew easily and plentifully in the central African soil. These new sources of food and income increased chances for central African groups to organize into social and political units. Small, often short-lived kingdoms such as the Azande and Ngbandi emerged in the region.

The slave trade had a devastating effect on the area. Not trusting outsiders, local groups such as the Sara, Banda, and Mboum tried to further isolate themselves. And slave raiders didn't just steal people from their homes. They also unknowingly introduced new diseases into the area. Central Africans had no natural immunity (resistance) to these diseases. Many died from smallpox, measles, and other illnesses.

By the mid-nineteenth century, the Bobangi people from the Oubangui River area had become slave traders themselves. They raided the nearby Baya and Mandija peoples. The new slaves were transported to the Atlantic coast, where they were handed over to slave brokers who sold the captives in overseas markets. This practice created intense anger between the groups. Deep resentments against the raiding groups grew.

African slave traders brought captives to slave ships, which transported them across the Atlantic.

Hoping to avoid capture, many Central Africans fled from their homes. Sometimes entire groups would migrate. They were especially watchful during the dry season, when slave raiders were most active and could travel more easily. This constant upheaval hampered the development of a strong social organization among the region's ethnic groups. Villages remained isolated from one another as the waves of raiders attempted to meet the increasing demand for slaves in other parts of the world.

The Oubangui-Chari Colony

By the end of the nineteenth century, the growing economy in the eastern area of present-day CAR had attracted European merchants. These traders hoped to gain access to wild rubber, ivory, and other resources in the region. The Europeans also wanted to find new markets for their goods.

Fast ships, powerful weapons, and quinine—a medicine that helps control a deadly disease called malaria—made it possible for Europeans to gain control of vast areas of Africa. The Industrial Revolution in Europe had created the need for more markets and for new sources of raw materials. European powers—including Belgium, Germany, Great Britain, and France—competed for control of African territories. French colonists arrived in the present-day Central African Republic in the late 1880s. They later named the colony Oubangui-Chari (also spelled Ubangi-Shari), after the two major river systems there.

The European powers worked out boundaries for Oubangui-Chari and other territories. The French established the city of Bangui in

Two **colonial French men** travel through the Central African Republic in the early twentieth century.

1889 as a capital. By the beginning of the twentieth century, colonial frontiers had been set for western and central Africa. (The colonists never bothered to consult the local people.) In 1910 the French added Oubangui-Chari to Gabon, Congo, and Chad, creating the federation of French Equatorial Africa (AEF, for the French abbreviation). Although a governor-general ruled the entire federation, a lieutenant governor living in Bangui had authority in Oubangui-Chari.

Many local peoples of the region resisted French control. They used methods such as work slowdowns, migration out of the region, and violence. One group that offered firm resistance was the Vridi, led by Baram-Bakie (a slave trader). From 1906 to 1909, the Vridi maintained control of a small portion of territory near the Oubangui River. But such resistance movements couldn't stand for long against the superior French forces.

The Effects of Colonization

After it had established control in the region, the French government profited from the colony by leasing large tracts of land to private European companies. Upon gaining a lease, a firm had almost complete power over the land and its people. Company overseers forced Central Africans—often by means of physical punishment—to collect rubber from the wild rubber trees that grew on the land and to sell their ivory to foreign merchants. In addition, family farms were absorbed into larger plantations, a development that caused further breakdowns in village life. To make things even worse, the region suffered from widespread famine and disease.

European politics set many colonial borders during the early twentieth century. As a result, portions of Oubangui-Chari were sometimes considered part of Congo or Cameroon. Furthermore, different European powers controlled areas of the Oubangui-Chari colony for various periods of time. For example, a western region called Neu Kamerun (New Cameroon) was in German

THE EVOLVED

The French colonial administration used the term *évolués* (evolved) to describe Africans who were educated and had adopted a Western (European-style) lifestyle. The évolués were given special privileges and had a greater ability to advance in the French-dominated social hierarchy. But not everyone respected the évolués. Barthélemy Boganda, a political leader of the late 1940s and 1950s, had a different, less flattering name for them—*mboundjou-voko* (white-blacks). It was Boganda's way of criticizing blacks who acted like whites.

hands from 1911 to 1914. World War I (1914–1918) drastically changed the political climate in Europe, however. France and Great Britain were among the countries fighting Germany, and after their victory, they took over many German-controlled lands in the area.

In the 1920s, the French government forced thousands of men from Oubangui-Chari to work on the Congo-Ocean Railroad. It was being built in the French colony of Congo, hundreds of miles from their homes. Many men refused to submit to forced labor. They staged several uprisings, which French troops quickly put down.

The region experienced little social, political, or educational development in the first decades of the twentieth century. In the late 1920s, the French began to create a health system in the colony to fight disease—especially sleeping sickness. Roman Catholic and Protestant missionaries (people who try to convert others to their faith) set up schools and medical clinics.

The French, meanwhile, were finding it hard to make Oubangui-Chari profitable. They tried to force farmers to grow cotton but never got the production they wanted. Coffee plantations might have been productive. But a crop disease destroyed many of the coffee trees in 1938. Only a gradual increase in gold and diamond production brought profit to French investors.

The Aftermath of World War II

With the outbreak of World War II (1939–1945), Germany and France (as well as other countries) were again at war. When Germany invaded France, French general Charles de Gaulle called for the help of French troops, European colonists, and residents of the colonies. Three thousand Central Africans fought on the side of the French in battles in North Africa, the Middle East, and Europe. After the war—won by France and its allies—many Baya, Mandija, and Banda troops returned to their homeland with a sense of national identity. They no longer regarded themselves only as members of separate ethnic communities. These war veterans had a wide awareness of the world and of the possibilities for their own region. A move toward national independence had begun.

In the late 1940s, the colony prospered under a French-appointed governor-general named Félix Éboué. Éboué had served in different positions within the colony for twenty years before assuming his high post. To give some authority to local people, he sought out African leaders and named them as administrators in the region.

With financial assistance from the United States, the French government launched a series of public projects in Oubangui-Chari. These improvements, along with increased investment in mining, led many

Colonial governor Félix Éboué and French general Charles de Gaulle attend a war time ceremony in neighboring Congo in 1944.

to believe that economic development might occur in the colony. But few Central Africans could afford to buy the products that the nation produced, so African farmers and workers had little reason to produce surplus (extra) goods. Demands on the world market for Oubangui-Chari products grew slowly, and only a few French settlers had enough money to invest in factories or in big farms.

In return for African help during the war, France began reforming the way it ran its African colonies. In 1946 France organized its holdings into the French Union. The French leadership created new territorial assemblies (legislatures). French colonists and some local Africans became regional representatives. A few Africans even participated in the French National Assembly (France's lawmaking government branch). On November 10, 1946, Barthélemy Boganda became the first Central African elected to the French legislature.

At first, the French granted voting rights in the newly established French Union to only a handful of educated Africans. But over time, more and more Africans gained the right to vote.

Barthélemy Boganda

A French-educated Roman Catholic priest, Boganda worked for reform within the French Union. After leaving the priesthood in 1949, Boganda

Barthélemy Boganda

formed the Movement for the Social Evolution of Black Africa (known by the French abbreviation MESAN). As a political party, MESAN united many Central Africans who were dissatisfied with French rule.

Boganda worked hard fighting for rights for the black Africans he represented. He helped end the forced labor practices that blacks had endured under the cotton producers and coffee plantation owners. He also introduced laws in the National Assembly in France to end discrimination in the territory's legal system and to decrease taxes that Africans had to pay. Boganda and MESAN did not focus too much on national independence, instead concentrating on expanding the rights of the people of Oubangui-Chari. Nevertheless, Boganda's efforts to change the government distressed many French colonists, who worried that their positions of profit and power would disappear as black Africans became empowered.

The Loi Cadre (basic law), which was passed in France in 1956, eliminated the final barriers to full voter participation in the territories. It also created government structures to help the colonies develop self-rule. Boganda and MESAN were so popular with Africans that the party won all the seats in the 1957 territorial assembly election. Boganda became president of the assembly.

The Road to Independence

The French government wanted the members of the French Union to evolve into a community of independent territories, with France as their leader. France looked to MESAN, headed by Boganda, to lead Oubangui-Chari to independence within such an organization.

In September 1958, the French dissolved French Equatorial Africa and increased the authority of the individual territories. The local governing bodies dealt with internal affairs, while France still controlled the territories' foreign relations. In December 1958, changes in the French constitution transformed the French Union into the French Community and allowed the territories even more self-rule.

The Oubangui-Chari territory officially became the autonomous (self-ruling) territory of the Central African Republic, with Boganda as its prime minister.

Boganda hoped that the former French territories of Chad, Gabon, Congo, and Oubangui-Chari could form a single nation. He had visions of an even larger grouping—the United States of Latin Africa—that would also include Zaire, Angola, and Cameroon. Boganda feared that landlocked CAR would have many economic difficulties if it became a separate country. But de Gaulle didn't like the idea of unification. He wanted to keep the territories dependent on France. When Gabon, Chad, and Congo rejected the plan to unify, Boganda led the CAR to accept the new constitution offered by France.

Boganda died in a plane crash on March 29, 1959. Many considered the circumstances of his death suspicious (several groups felt threatened by his policies, most notably French landowners in the CAR, and may have been involved in his death). The territorial assembly chose David Dacko, a former schoolteacher and Boganda's nephew, as the new president, selecting him over Boganda's longtime assistant Abel Goumba. Under Dacko, the Central African Republic finally achieved full independence (with the blessing of the French) on August 13, 1960.

Dacko and Bokassa

After the Central African Republic achieved independence, Dacko and a small group of French-supported Central Africans gained complete power in the new nation. Dacko's rule was a dictatorship. He was intolerant of any opposition. He had police arrest Goumba, who had tried to set up an opposing political party. In 1962 Dacko officially made MESAN the nation's only legal political party. Without opposition, he was formally elected president in 1964. A few months later, the MESAN candidates won all sixy seats in the elections for the National Assembly.

Although the Central African Republic was independent, Dacko made international agreements that gave France broad authority in trade, defense, and foreign relations. He also added more and more highly paid government positions to reward his supporters. These actions, along with further government corruption, drove the young

David Dacko

CAR into an economic crisis. Soon the nation could not pay its workers. A nationwide strike loomed.

On December 31, 1965, Jean-Bedel Bokassa—the commander of the army—led a nearly bloodless coup (a swift, forceful overthrow of a government). Dacko fled to Europe. Bokassa and his supporters took over important governmental positions, defeating opposition wherever it formed. He suspended the nation's constitution and dissolved the National Assembly. He often took a direct role in crushing opposition by assisting the police and army as they arrested, questioned, and sometimes beat prisoners. Despite Bokassa's harsh rule, France supported him and the faltering economy. The French did so because they wanted to retain access to the country's diamond mines and to its potential uranium supply.

Bokassa's Central African Empire

Bokassa wasn't content merely being president. In 1976 he proclaimed himself emperor of the nation, which he renamed the Central African Empire. The crowning took place in December 1977. The

Self-proclaimed emperor Jean-Bedel Bokassa sits on his throne during his coronation ceremony on December 4, 1977.

French government financed and organized much of the costly coronation ceremonies. Almost half of the annual income of the Central African Empire was spent on the ceremony. The poor of the country grew poorer still as Bokassa and his supporters lived like kings.

Under Bokassa's rule, the government went further into debt. The emperor rewarded those who supported him by giving them government positions and by increasing the salaries of those he already employed. Bokassa personally administered the nation's diamond trade and took most of the profits for himself. The cost of consumer goods rose, while the quality of basic services declined. More and more, the nation's economy depended on aid from France.

In January 1979, Emperor Bokassa ordered all high school students to wear uniforms made in one of his factories. This led to student demonstrations in Bangui against the emperor. Bokassa called out the army to subdue the crowd. One of the darkest times in the history of the nation came in April 1979. After a group of protesting youths threw stones at the car of Bokassa, the emperor became enraged. He ordered a massive roundup of children and adolescents. Over the next two nights, Bokassa was involved in the murder of about one hundred children. The event would become known as the Children's Massacre at Bangui.

A panel of Central African judges charged Bokassa with murder. France acted quickly, suddenly throwing its support back to Dacko. Bokassa responded by flying to Libya to ask for assistance from Muammar al-Qaddafi—the Libyan head of state and France's enemy. In September 1979, the French flew Dacko from Europe into Bangui, along with French troops from Gabon and Chad. Within hours this French-backed coup had deposed Bokassa. Dacko was restored as president, and the nation's name changed back to the Central African Republic. Bokassa, meanwhile, fled the country and eventually settled in France. (He later returned to the CAR, only to be arrested and sentenced to death for his crimes—a sentence later reduced to life in prison.)

Power Struggles

The people of the CAR were not enthusiastic about Dacko's return to power. Active opposition to his rule soon emerged from students and

---

CULT OF PERSONALITY

Emperor Bokassa worked to build a larger-than-life image of himself. He wanted the people of the CAR to revere him. Music was one tool he used to build his image. He built a large recording studio and gave money to many popular bands and musicians. In return, the bands and musicians sang his praises as a great leader.

throngs of unemployed workers in Bangui. Dacko relied on the French military presence to hold his position. In turn, France pressured Dacko to promote democracy. Dacko called for a new constitution and held elections in early 1981. Dacko won the election. But governmental interference and obvious vote fraud caused many Central Africans to doubt that the results were accurate.

Labor strikes and bomb attacks undermined Dacko's control within the country. Dacko increasingly began to rely on the army to keep hold of power. On September 1, 1981, General André Kolingba led a coup that removed Dacko from office. Kolingba set up a military government, headed by his Military Committee for National Recovery. As the CAR's new leader, Kolingba said that he would try both to strengthen the economy (by requesting more aid from neighboring states and from France) and establish a democratic government. He vowed to stamp out corruption and to reduce the size of the bloated CAR government.

André Kolingba

Many of the civil servants (government employees) from Bokassa's and Dacko's administrations remained, however. And the level of corruption only grew. In addition, despite his promise to establish democracy, Kolingba delayed elections year after year. Throughout the late 1980s, Kolingba's government faced public pressure to allow more than one political party.

The Central African government stayed in the hands of the military until 1985. In that year, Kolingba dissolved the military committee and named a new cabinet that included civilians. In early 1986, under international pressure, the re-formed National Assembly passed a new constitution that called for legislative elections. But Kolingba remained firmly in power.

In 1991 the National Assembly revised the constitution in accordance with the demands for a multiparty system. The following year, Central African political leaders participated in a Grand National Debate to change the constitution. They separated the legislative, executive, and judicial branches of government. They agreed that elections would take place for a new, multiparty legislative body. Kolingba was to rule until the elections could be held. Kolingba managed to delay elections until 1993, when voters chose new legislators and elected former prime minister Ange-Felix Patassé to the presidency.

Patassé's Struggles

The people of the CAR were ready for change, and Patassé wanted to lead them to a more democratic state. But he stepped into a difficult situation. The country's economy was in ruins. The treasury had no money to pay civil servants or members of the military.

Public employees had long been dissatisfied with the government's failure to pay their salaries completely and on time. This resentment came to a head in 1996. Central African soldiers, angry because they had not been paid for months, rose up against the government and demanded that Patassé be removed from office. The soldiers took control of Bangui, looting and damaging much of the city and killing many of its people. Foreign peacekeeping forces—first from France and neighboring nations and later from the United Nations (UN)—tried to keep order in the faltering country.

French soldiers patrol a main street in Bangui following widespread looting and antigovernment unrest in 1996.

CAR president **Ange-Felix Patassé** waves to a crowd in Bangui shortly before his reelection as president in 1999.

The situation was so bad that Patassé created a new police force called the Squad for the Repression of Banditry. He allowed for the execution of criminals just a day after their arrest, without any kind of fair trial. Despite all of these problems, Patassé won reelection in 1999.

▶ A New Century

The political situation in the CAR didn't improve with the new century. UN peacekeeping forces pulled out of the country in 2000. With the international forces gone, Kolingba led a May 2001 coup attempt. After several bloody days of fighting, Patassé's forces put down the coup attempt. But the political instability was far from over. In November 2001, François Bozizé (the former chief of staff of the armed forces) began to take control of some CAR lands. Bozizé finally ousted Patassé from power in March 2003, with the help of Libyan troops.

Bozizé worked quickly to seize control of the country. He oversaw the drafting of a new constitution in 2004. Promising change,

François Bozizé (left) walks through army headquarters in Bangui with military leaders from Chad after taking control of the CAR in 2003.

he was formally elected president in 2005. He vowed to reunite a divided country but inherited many of the problems that had prevented previous leaders from doing so—especially the nation's wrecked economy.

Rebel opposition in the northeast, where support for Patassé was strong, hampered Bozizé's government in 2006. Rebel forces captured the northeastern town of Birao in December 2006 and then again in March 2007. Bozizé and the French bombed the town to drive out the rebels, destroying as much of 80 percent of Birao in the process. Hundreds of thousands of people became refugees as they were caught in the crossfire between government and rebel forces. Many of these people fled

"We could see the villages burning and the children were screaming and really scared, so we ran two kilometres [1.2 miles] out into the jungle. From there we could see our whole city on fire. We fled along the river and stayed out there. We ate fish, but there weren't many. Some days we couldn't catch anything and we starved. The children were so terrified. Still, when they hear a loud noise, they think there are guns coming and they start shaking."

—Idris, a Central African, on the March 2006 bombing of Birao

"Bozizé is burning our villages. A country shouldn't burn its own country's villages. It is like a mother and a child, a mother does not burn her child, it would be madness."

—resistance leader Laurent Djim-Woei, on the Bozizé government in the CAR

into Chad and Cameroon. Others lived in inadequate, makeshift shelters, afraid to return to their homes.

The troubles of the CAR carried into 2008, with no end in sight. Rebel groups continued to cause problems for Bozizé, while bandits in rural areas made travel dangerous. Violence in the nearby country of Sudan also spilled over across CAR borders. Meanwhile, in January, the nation's teachers and civil servants staged a strike to protest that they weren't being paid. As a result, Prime Minister Elie Dote resigned in January 2008. Bozizé named Faustin Archange Touadera as his successor.

CAR troops guard an airstrip in February 2007 that had been held by rebels.

Government

The constitution of the CAR has been written, discarded, rewritten, and revised time and again throughout its short history as an independent nation. The most recent version of the constitution was drafted in 2004. It places the president as the head of state and leader of the executive branch. The president is elected by a democratic vote and can serve a maximum of two five-year terms. The CAR has universal suffrage, which means that all adults aged twenty-one and older can vote. The president appoints the prime minister, who serves as the official head of the government, as well as a Council of Ministers (a team of advisers heading various government agencies).

The CAR's legislative branch is the 109-member National Assembly. Assembly members are elected to five-year terms, based on their political parties' percentage of votes. For example, if a party earned 50 percent of the national vote, it would get half of the seats in the legislature. The Movement for the Liberation of the Central African People (MLPC) is the National Assembly's dominant party.

The country's system of courts is based loosely on the French judicial system. The Supreme Court is the highest court in the land. It consists of nine judges. The president appoints three judges, the National Assembly three, and fellow judges the final three. Other courts include the criminal courts and the Court of Appeals.

The CAR is split into sixteen prefectures (similar to states) and the commune of Bangui (similar to a township), each with their own local governments. The prefectures are further divided into seventy-one subprefectures (similar to counties).

THE ELEPHANTS AND THE GRASS

The Central African people have paid a heavy price because of all the nation's political turmoil. Because of this, many people have an indifferent outlook about their leaders. A popular proverb (saying) reflects this view: "When the elephants fight, the grass suffers; when the elephants make love, the grass still suffers." In the proverb, the elephants represent the leaders, while the grass represents the people.

Visit www.vgsbooks.com for links to websites with current information on the state of government and level of unrest in the Central African Republic.

THE PEOPLE

With only 4.3 million people, the Central African Republic is a sparsely populated country. Its population density of 18 people per square mile (7 people per sq. km) is among the lowest in Africa. In addition, the distribution of people in the country is very uneven. High concentrations of the CAR's people live in settlements along the Oubangui River and near the borders with Chad and Cameroon, while the country's eastern regions are much more sparsely populated.

Like most other African nations, the CAR has a large rural population, with roughly 62 percent of its people residing in the countryside. The CAR also has a population dominated by the young, with 43 percent of Central Africans below the age of fifteen. At its current rate of growth, the nation's population in 2050 will be about 7.6 million.

◗ Ethnic Groups

The CAR has seven main ethnic groups, as well as many subgroupings and smaller groups. Ethnicity in the CAR isn't always a simple matter,

however. Ethnic groupings are often artificial, with plenty of crossover from one group to the next. In addition, getting accurate population figures for many peoples is difficult. Many live in remote areas, and some tend to avoid the census (official population count) because they associate it with taxation or forced labor.

The largest ethnic group is the Baya, making up 33 percent of the population. The Baya are often grouped with the Mandija, who represent another 13 percent of Central Africans. When considered together, these two similar groups are called the Baya-Mandija.

The Baya-Mandija are mainly farmers. They are centered in the southwest and spread across the borders into Cameroon, the Republic of the Congo, and the DRC. The Baya-Mandija arrived in the region in the early 1800s, fleeing northern Cameroon, where the slave trade was much more active. Former president Ange-Felix Patassé is a member of the Suma, one of the many subgroups of the Baya-Mandija.

The Banda represent 27 percent of the CAR's population. The Banda live mainly in the central parts of the country but spread into the south, as well as into Cameroon, the Republic of the Congo, and the DRC. Like the Baya, they settled in the present-day CAR in the early 1800s while fleeing slave raiders. Polygamy (men having more than one wife) was once common among the Banda, but the practice has fallen off in modern times. The Banda generally live in small savanna hamlets (towns) under the control of a single headman. The men hunt and fish, while the women tend to crops.

The Sara make up about 10 percent of the population. The Sara are descended from the Sao people of Chad and are settled mainly in the northwestern part of the country. Like the Banda, the Sara practice polygamy, and many of the people have held on to traditional religions.

The remaining three major ethnic groups in the CAR are the Mboum (7 percent), M'Baka (4 percent), and the Yakoma (4 percent). The Mboum live mainly near the Cameroon border. The M'Baka tend to live alongside rivers. They make up only a small minority of Central Africans but have provided the country with many of its leaders, including Boganda, Dacko, and Bokassa. This is largely because they were among the first people contacted by Europeans and benefited the most from Western education. The Yakoma, meanwhile, live along the Oubangui River. Many of them make their living trading up and down the river and its tributaries. Former president Kolingba is of the Yakoma people.

Other groups make up the remaining 2 percent of the CAR's population. This includes Europeans—mainly French—still living in the area, as well as refugees from Chad, Sudan, and other countries. The Aka and Baka are also included in this total. These nomadic forest people are known for their small stature and powerful vocal musical style.

THE AKA

The Aka is an ethnic group that almost defies classification by region or speech. The Aka, or pygmies, are generally people of very small stature. Many stand no more than 4 feet (1.2 meters) tall. Their small size makes the Aka well adapted to move quickly and easily through their traditional lands in the southwestern rain forests of the CAR. These people travel from place to place searching for edible plants and prey. The term *pygmy* was once considered disrespectful, but many modern-day members of the Aka (and the closely related Baka and Twa peoples) embrace it.

Language

With its variety of ethnic groups, the CAR is a land of many languages. Two tongues—French and Sango—dominate and are the national languages. French came to the region in the late 1800s. As France's power in the region grew, French became a language of privilege and elevated social class. Those who learned the language had more opportunities to move up the social ladder. In modern times, French remains the main language used in education, international business, and government.

Sango is the lingua franca (common language) of the CAR. Sango originated in the Oubangui River region, but it has been heavily pidginized (changed and simplified) so that it is easily learned and spoken by people all across the country.

WHERE DID SANGO COME FROM?

The origin of the Sango language is a matter of debate. One idea is that it started from an Oubanguian language called Ngbandi. People who speak this language are able to understand Sango even if they've never heard it before. But the reverse isn't true. Sango speakers who don't speak Ngbandi aren't able to understand the language.

Signs in the CAR are commonly written in French. This sign encourages AIDS awareness.

Sango is a language of great variation, however. The Sango spoken in remote rural areas may bear little resemblance to that spoken in Bangui, for example. Furthermore, in some areas, it has been somewhat blended with French, with speakers mixing and matching elements from the two languages almost interchangeably.

Many ethnic groups speak their own languages as well. The CAR's almost 70 indigenous (local) languages can be grouped into four main language families: Nilo-Saharen, Bantu, Adamawan, and Oubanguian. Nilo-Saharen is common in the north, stretching across the borders with Sudan and Chad. Bantu languages prevail in the southwest, while the Adamawan tongues are found in the northwest. The broad Oubanguian family, which includes Sango, is most prominent and spans most of the country.

CENTRAL AFRICAN STYLE

The people of the CAR dress in both traditional African and Western styles *(below)*. Traditional clothing for both men and women includes *pagnes*. These lengths of fabric are wrapped around the waist or the chest. Like much traditional African clothing, they are often brightly colored and embroidered in complex patterns. The Western influence is especially strong in the business world. Men wear loose three-piece suits, while women wear skirts, dresses, or pants.

◉ Daily Life

Most Central Africans continue to live off the land. They practice age-old agricultural techniques using hand tools and have little money with which to make farming improvements (such as buying tractors). Many Central Africans remain unable to raise enough nutritious food to feed their families.

Most Central Africans launder their clothes on the banks of streams, spreading their garments out on the ground to dry in the sunlight. Often with babies strapped to their backs, rural women

Because few Central Africans can afford motorized vehicles, **walking is a major form of transportation,** especially in rural areas.

work throughout the day. They transport loads of firewood or containers of water on their heads. Women also grow the bulk of the nation's food. Most of the men cultivate crops that will be exported—such as coffee, cotton, and tobacco—or they hunt and fish to supply food. They may also tend livestock.

Urban dwellers may work in factories, government centers, on the streets as vendors, or in other jobs. Their lifestyles vary widely based on their income. The poor may live in *kodros*. Kodros are almost like tight-knit small villages within a city, often including people of similar ethnic backgrounds. Like in rural villages, the homes of most poor urban dwellers lack modern conveniences such as electricity and running water. These luxuries are limited to the small number of wealthy Central Africans living mainly in Bangui.

The CAR is a male-dominated society. For the most part, women are expected to tend to the home and the family. Husbands expect their wives to be obedient and often forbid them from working outside the home (although most street vendors tend to be women). The education of girls is valued less than that of boys, leading to lower literacy rates and fewer opportunities for females. Despite these barriers, some women do rise to power in the CAR, in business as well as government. Most notably, Elisabeth Domitien served as the nation's prime minister from 1975 to 1976.

Health

Most of the CAR lacks modern medical facilities. Bangui is the only place that consistently has a full range of medical supplies on hand, including the nation's only major hospital. Simple herbal treatments are all many rural Central Africans can hope to get for their ailments.

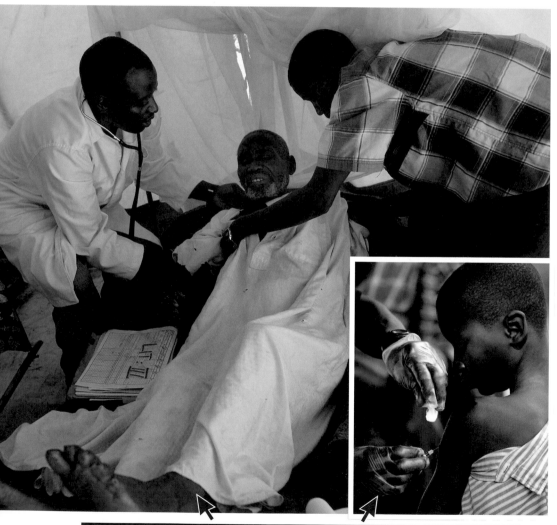

Above: Medical staff at a Doctors Without Borders clinic in the CAR treat a sick man. *Inset:* A boy receives a vaccination for measles after an outbreak in his city. Diseases that are easily treated or avoided in North America and Europe are dangers in the CAR due to the CAR's lack of medical services and safe water.

As a result, the nation has one of the world's lowest life expectancy rates, at just 43 years (42 years for men and 45 years for women). Infant mortality rates are also high, at 102 deaths per 1,000 births.

Many other factors contribute to the generally poor health of people in the CAR. Unsafe supplies of water, poor sanitation, and malnutrition (the lack of enough food or nutrients) afflict children and adults alike. Diseases such as malaria, typhoid fever, leprosy, tuberculosis, and hepatitis are widespread, further straining what few medical facilities the nation has.

A still greater problem is the human immunodeficiency virus (HIV), which leads to acquired immunodeficiency syndrome (AIDS). This deadly virus, which is spread mostly through sexual contact, afflicts 6.2 percent of the nation's adult population. The nation lacks the medical facilities to treat its high number of AIDS patients, and modern medicines to control the disease are generally unavailable.

SLEEPING SICKNESS

Sleeping sickness, or African trypanosomiasis, is a dangerous disease spread by the tsetse fly. Early symptoms include fever, headache, and joint pain. In time, the glands often swell up to enormous size. The disease soon spreads into the brain. Two of the effects are extreme fatigue during the day (giving the disease its name) and insomnia at night. Left untreated, the disease is fatal. An epidemic of the disease broke out in Africa in 1970 and is still going on. As many as seventy thousand people in sub-Saharan Africa (the part of Africa south of the Sahara) may be infected. With its many tsetse flies and lack of medical facilities, the CAR is one of the most vulnerable countries to the disease.

Tsetse flies, which look like large houseflies, infest much of the country. The insect's bite transmits parasites that carry disease into the bloodstream of the bitten person or animal. Tsetse flies infect humans with a deadly disease called sleeping sickness (it also infects cattle and horses with a similar disease called nagana). The insects are so bad in some areas that settlement is almost impossible. International organizations are exploring ways to chemically control the tsetse fly population across Africa, but progress is slow.

Visit www.vgsbooks.com for links to websites with more information on the health challenges facing the CAR. Learn more about the daily life of people in the CAR.

◉ Education

Until 1953 the French colonial government of the CAR did not pro-vide educational opportunities beyond the elementary level. High school education in the CAR was offered only in schools established by Christian missionaries. Most public schools were poorly equipped and had few teachers. The first publicly funded high school was estab-lished in 1953, and its first class graduated in 1956.

After independence in 1960, the government of the CAR spent more than 20 percent of its budget on education, and the number of schools and students increased rapidly. By the 1990s, educational spending had tumbled to less than 3 percent due to the poor economy and political unrest, and the quality and availability of public educa-tion fell sharply.

Education in the CAR still faces many challenges. Most classes are taught in French, but more and more are switching to Sango. Children ages six through fourteen are required by law to go to school. However, as many as 75 percent of eligible children do not attend regular classes, staying at home to work to help support their families. This is especially true among girls. Schools suffer from overcrowding, understaffing, and a lack of resources. These challenges contribute to the nation's overall literacy rate of just 51 percent. Men fare somewhat better than women, however. About 63 percent of CAR men can read and write, compared to just 40 percent of women. Figures for both men and women are, however, on the rise.

A boy writes in French on a blackboard at his school in the bush (countryside). **The bush system** was created to educate children displaced by violence in the CAR.

A teacher reads to his class at a community school. Most classes in the CAR are severely overcrowded and underequipped.

The University of Bangui, founded by Jean-Bedel Bokassa, has operated on an irregular basis since it opened in 1967. Students study law, economics, science, and more. In the late 1980s, the university went through a large expansion. It added a college of education, the University Institute of Mines and Geology, the National School of Administration, the School of Arts and Crafts, a medical school, and the National School of Agriculture. The CAR also has several religious educational institutions. Many young people of wealthy families pursue studies abroad, often in France.

CULTURAL LIFE

The Central African Republic is home to many different ethnic groups and belief systems. For thousands of years, separate cultures remained fairly isolated. But in the modern world, they blend—and sometimes clash—creating a unique and varied national culture. Traditional African stories, music, language, and religion have mixed with European—especially French—culture. The result is a culture that is uniquely Central African.

Folktales and Literature

The people of the present-day CAR had no system of reading and writing before Arab and European people arrived. But they did have a rich tradition of oral history and folktales, sometimes called *orature*. Storytelling was an important part of village life. At night, people often gathered around a fire as elders told stories of history, spirituality, group beliefs, and more. Storytelling was truly a communal affair. One person might begin a familiar tale, only to have another—or sev-

eral others—finish it. The stories carried on from generation to generation, preserving a group's history even if it wasn't written down.

Europeans introduced writing to the region. Using the Roman
alphabet, Europeans wrote down some of the indigenous languages.
They created dictionaries and grammar books. Soon some Central
Africans learned to read and write in their own languages.

In modern times, the CAR has not produced a great deal of published literature and has few authors of note. Its best-known author is
Pierre Makombo Bamboté. His novels, *Daba's Travels from Ouadda
to Bangui* (1971) and *Princess Mandapu* (1972) are set in the CAR and
have earned him some acclaim. He also published a collection of short
stories titled *News of Bangui*.

Other authors of note include Pierre Sammy Mackfoy and Etienne
Goyemide. Sammy Mackfoy has written a series of works center-
ing on a character named Mongou. They include *Mongou, Son of
Bandia* (1967), *The Odyssey of Mongou* (1983), *The Blue Butterfly and*

RESPECTING THE ELDERS

Central Africans revere and respect their elders. The elderly are seen as being close to the ancestors whom people honor through their traditional religions. They are valued for their wisdom and experience. The elderly help settle disputes, make major family decisions, and delight the young with stories and folktales.

the *Daughter of the Devil* (1989), and *The Illusions of Mongou* (2002). Goyemide's *The Silence of the Forest* (2003) is about a man who gives up his modern life to live in the forest with the pygmies.

Poetry is a popular form of writing among many Central Africans. Aristide Mblanendji Ndakala is among the nation's greatest poets. Ndakala combines traditional forms with his own writing style. His collection, *Poems for Liberation* (2005), evokes a sense of beauty for the African landscape and an awareness of its deep history.

▶ Religion

The CAR is home to a rich religious diversity, including Western religions, indigenous beliefs, and unique combinations of the two. The nation is tolerant of all faiths. Members of different religions are expected to live and work side by side. In fact, in Bangui, it's common to see Christian churches standing alongside Islamic mosques. Many people adopt elements of different faiths.

Two men stand in front of a Roman Catholic church in Bossangoa. About 50 percent of people in the CAR are Christians.

About 50 percent of Central Africans identify themselves as Christians. Of these, the numbers are about evenly split between Roman Catholics and Protestants. Missionaries brought Christianity to the region in the late 1800s. The faith flourished under French control, when Westernizing offered extra benefits to local peoples.

Another 35 percent of Central Africans follow indigenous beliefs. These wide-ranging religions existed long before the arrival of Europeans and have survived—and thrived—into the twenty-first century. Individual belief systems vary, but many include common elements. Ancestor worship is one such element. Many Central Africans believe that the spirits of their ancestors can impact their daily lives. They revere their dead and even offer small items to the spirits of their ancestors. Animism is another part of many belief systems. Animism is the belief that animals, plants, and even objects have spirits of their own, and that they can affect the day-to-day world. Many indigenous belief systems also include magic and witchcraft. Some villages have their own witch doctors, who use herbal mixtures and magic to tend to the sick. Even many people who practice Christianity or Islam maintain some indigenous beliefs. The combination of belief systems is often called syncreticism.

The remaining 15 percent of Central Africans follow Islam, a religion founded on the Arabian Peninsula in the A.D. 600s. Most of the CAR's Muslims are of the Sunni branch. Hundreds of years ago, many Central Africans distrusted Muslims. They associated Islam with the Arab slave raiders who stole people from their homes. For this reason, the faith has only recently taken hold in the region. Muslims follow the teachings of the prophet Muhammad. He founded the faith on the Arabian Peninsula in the seventh century. Muslims believe that Allah (Arabic for "God") revealed his teachings to

SLEEPING WITH THE SPIRITS

Many of the indigenous religions of the CAR focus on the presence of spirits. People believe that spirits—good and evil—affect the everyday world. According to indigenous beliefs, people interact with spirits while sleeping—a state thought of as half-death. During sleep, a person's soul leaves the body and travels, sometimes meeting spirits. A person who dies in his or her sleep is believed to have been killed by an evil spirit.

Many people of the CAR wear small charms, or fetishes. Wearers believe that the charms ward off witches, bring good luck, or have other magical powers.

The large white building on the edge of Bouar is a **mosque** (Islamic house of worship).

Muhammad. These revelations are collected in a holy book called the Quran. The deeds and sayings of Muhammad are collected in a book called the Hadith. Together, the books provide spiritual, political, and legal guides to believers.

Art

Until the nineteenth century, craftspeople in the region produced many fine handmade items, such as decorative pottery, intricately woven mats, fine-tooled leather goods, musical instruments, and handsome textiles. The slave trade and the early years of colonization disrupted the expansion of crafts, however, and many of them disappeared. By the late 1980s, roughly woven mats and baskets, simple wooden utensils, and plain pottery were all that remained of traditional local handiwork. Slowly, traditional crafts are returning, however. One interesting craft is the creation of unique designs and pictures made from butterfly wings glued to paper.

Modern Central African artists produce both watercolor and oil paintings. The murals and canvasses of Jérôme Ramedane depict scenes of African animal life, hunting parties, and daily village life. Similar works are often found on the walls of restaurants, bars, and other gathering places in Bangui and large villages.

Music and Dance

From traditional sounds to contemporary hits, Central Africans have a love affair with music. Music is almost a way of life. It accompanies ritual, religion, social gatherings, and even everyday tasks.

Traditional Central African music makes use of many instruments. The heavy beat of drums is a big part of the traditional sound. The xylophone and its close relative the *balafon* are other popular percussion instruments. Horns, a wide variety of stringed instruments, and voices fill out the sound. Complex vocal harmonies are especially important in traditional pygmy music.

Contemporary music in the CAR fuses traditional sounds with modern styles, including soul, funk, salsa, and dance. Guitars, keyboards, and other modern instruments create a blend that is uniquely Central African. Likewise, song lyrics often reflect the situation of the Central African people. Much contemporary music has a political aspect. Performers sing about the AIDS crisis, racism, poverty, and more.

Like music, dance permeates the Central African culture. It is a group activity, whether in ritual or in the hopping nightclubs of Bangui. Many dances have a spiritual meaning for Central Africans. For example, the *nbakia* dance of the Bandia honors the dancers' ancestors. Pygmy dancers mimic the motions of animals in the forest or of hunters. Among some forest dwellers, four days of dancing follow the killing of a leopard—an animal seen as a human killer.

 Visit www.vgsbooks.com for links to websites to read more about the culture of the Central African Republic.

Traditional dancers perform during an inauguration celebration in Bangui.

Media

In a nation with low literacy rates and a lack of a developed transportation system, newspapers do not play a role in the daily lives of most Central Africans. Most newspapers are printed in French, with a small amount of Sango content also appearing. The government-run *Centrafrique Presse* offers a limited viewpoint on current events. A handful of privately owned papers give more balanced coverage, but in many cases, their publication is irregular. Privately owned newspapers include *Le Citoyen, L'Echo de Centrafrique,* and *Le Novateur.*

Broadcast media—especially radio—play a much bigger role throughout the country. Most villages have at least one battery-operated radio. Listeners can tune into the state-run station Radio Centrafrique (also called Radio Bangui). This station offers music, some news, and various other programming. One of its most popular shows is called *Special Communications.* On this show, listeners in Bangui can send out greetings and messages to friends and family in rural areas. Another state-run station, Radio Rural, broadcasts entirely in Sango and is aimed at the rural population. Two other stations in Bangui are Radio Notre Dame, a Roman Catholic station, and Radio Ndeke Luka, backed by the United Nations. Depending on their location, listeners may also be able to tune in the British Broadcasting Corporation (BBC), Radio France Internationale, and Africa Number One, a station broadcast out of Gabon.

The state also runs a TV station, Television Centrafricaine (TVCA). But few CAR residents can afford televisions—or even have electrical service—to receive the broadcasts.

Holidays and Celebrations

Central Africans look forward to the country's many holidays as days of celebration and rest. Many of the CAR's national holidays celebrate its independence and leaders, including Republic Day on December 1, when people gather to listen to speeches from government leaders and to watch military parades. Central Africans celebrate the anniversary of the formation of the CAR government on May 15. March 29 is Boganda Day. Each year on this day, Central Africans honor one of their greatest leaders on the anniversary of his death.

Central Africans also celebrate major religious holidays. Officially, the government recognizes only Christian holidays such as Christmas and Easter. But members of other religions are also free to celebrate. For example, the nation's Muslims observe the month of Ramadan. During this month, Muslims fast (refrain from eating or drinking) during the daylight hours. Eid al-Fitr is a celebration feast that ends the

Cheerleaders march in a rally celebrating **Republic Day** in Bangui.

fast of Ramadan. Islamic holidays follow a lunar (moon) calendar, so holidays change dates and even seasons over time.

Smaller village celebrations are also common. These gatherings are often spontaneous. Villagers may celebrate the birth of a child or may just gather as members of a church. The people dress in their finest clothes and enjoy a feast of food and drink. They may talk, listen to music, and dance.

Sports

The people of the CAR work hard to carve out a life for themselves. Leisure time is often rare. But what free time people do have is often filled with sports.

Football (soccer) is by far the nation's most popular sport, both to play and to watch. Soccer fields are filled with children both in Bangui as well as in rural villages. Church and school teams are common for both boys and girls. Crowds gather to watch teams play at Barthélemy Boganda Stadium in Bangui.

Other popular sports in the CAR include basketball and rugby. Among the wealthy, exclusive sports clubs are popular. These expensive clubs are far beyond the reach of most Central Africans. The wealthy enjoy golf, tennis, horseback riding, and other sports there.

Central African athletes have competed at the Olympic Games, though not with a great deal of success. Track and field events, archery, judo, and taekwondo are a few of the events in which CAR athletes have competed. In the 2004 Summer Olympics in Athens, Greece, runner Ernest Ndjissipou finished the men's marathon in 2:21:23, good for 44th place overall.

Food

Central Africans live on a rich, fertile land. In the river valleys in the south and west, farmers grow millet (a cereal grain) and cassava to provide food for the nation's inhabitants. A plant with strong stalks and a large head of grain, millet grows 5 to 6 feet (1.5 to 1.8 m) tall. After workers harvest the crop and pound the grain in a large tub with a wooden hammer, millet can be made into porridge or fermented into a slightly alcoholic drink.

Cassavas measure from one to two feet (0.3 to 0.6 m) in length and resemble potatoes. Central Africans often use cassavas to make a sour, doughlike loaf. Central Africans have developed a way of drying cassava. After workers soften the root by pounding it, they grate the cassavas and spread out the small pieces to dry in the sun. The final product is a coarse flour. Dried cassava stays fresh for weeks and is easy to transport.

These starchy foods, along with corn and beans, are the staples of the Central African diet. Fruits and vegetables—including bananas, plantains (a fruit similar to a banana), lemons, yams, eggplant, hot

A group of farmers discuss their yam crop. Two baskets of yams sit in front of them.

SPINACH STEW

Meat is a luxury for most Central Africans. Many dishes, such as this spinach stew, contain only vegetables and grains. In the CAR, this thick, flavorful stew might be served with rice.

2 tablespoons vegetable oil	1 teaspoon salt
2 small onions, finely chopped	½ tablespoon cayenne pepper
1 green bell pepper, chopped	4 tablespoons peanut butter
2 tomatoes, peeled and sliced	4 tablespoons water
2 pounds fresh spinach, chopped	

1. Heat oil in large skillet or stewpot. Add onions and sauté until golden.
2. Add green bell pepper and tomatoes, and stir for 1 minute
3. Add spinach, salt, and cayenne pepper. Cover, reduce heat, and let simmer for 5 minutes.
4. Thin the peanut butter with the water, and mix to make a smooth paste. Add the paste to the skillet or pot.
5. Cook on low heat for 10 to 15 minutes, stirring frequently. If the stew begins to stick to the bottom of the pan, add small amounts of water and stir.
6. Serve alone or with rice.

Serves 6

peppers, spinach, and squash—add variety. *Foutou* is one common plantain dish. Plantains and cassavas are boiled and mashed into a smooth paste. The paste is rolled into balls and topped with an egg-plant sauce.

For many Central Africans, meat is a luxury served only on special occasions. Beef, pork, chicken, and mutton (sheep meat) are common meats, while fish is abundant in the nation's many rivers. Because meat is expensive, Central Africans make use of all they can. Children may eat chicken feet, for example, or suck the marrow out of the bones.

The most commonly served drink with a meal is water. But fruit juice, coffee, and tea also find their way onto some tables. Alcoholic drinks in the CAR include a ginger beer, palm wine, and *hydromel*, a honey-based beverage.

THE ECONOMY

Although the CAR contains a wealth of natural resources, the nation's economy struggles to grow. Several factors hamper development, including political instability, the lack of a seaport, undeveloped infrastructure, and foreign control over what resources do exist. Much of the country's wealth flows to France, Belgium, and other countries, doing little to benefit the people of the CAR.

The Central African Republic's unit of currency, the CFA franc, is also used by several other nations in the region, including Cameroon, Chad, Republic of the Congo, Equatorial Guinea, and Gabon. In early 1994, the French government, together with world financial institutions, forced nations using the CFA franc to decrease its value by half. The move was meant to control inflation (rising prices) but only served to further impoverish the CAR people.

The nation's gross domestic product (GDP)—the total of all goods and services produced within the country in one year—is $3.1 billion and is growing at a rate of about 4 percent per year. The

average income in the country is about $350 per year. But that average is highly skewed by a select class of the very wealthy. The average worker earns even less than that. The nation's unemployment is at 8 percent, though that number soars to 21 percent in Bangui.

Agriculture, Forestry, and Fishing

Agriculture is the basis of the Central African economy. This sector includes subsistence farming (raising only enough food to feed a family), commercial farming, forestry, and fishing. Agriculture makes up 55 percent of the CAR's GDP and employs an overwhelming majority of its workforce. About 10 percent of the country's area is suitable for farming, but only a fraction of that land is farmed. Nonresident foreigners own large acreages of land, which they use mainly as hunting reserves. These holdings, though fertile, remain undeveloped.

Subsistence farming is by far the most common type of agriculture. Most Central Africans live in rural villages and cultivate temporary

Villagers sit on the **cotton** they have picked. Farmers have a hard time making cotton profitable because what little machinery they do have is outdated.

fields. They clear the land of trees and brush by using the slash-and-burn technique before planting crops. After just a few years, the soil becomes depleted of its nutrients, and the farmers move on to other areas, where they repeat the process. These farmers raise food crops to feed their families, including cassava, corn, millet, peanuts, and rice. Cassava is the biggest staple, as it is easily grown. But it provides little nutritional value, leading to widespread malnutrition.

French plantation owners introduced the nation's two main export crops—coffee and cotton—in the 1920s. Present-day producers of these crops have had difficulty increasing crop volumes because they have little money to spend on replacing outdated equipment. Farmers are slowly developing new export crops, however, including palm oil, tobacco, and sugarcane.

Livestock in the CAR includes cattle, sheep, pigs, goats, chickens, and turkeys. Many animals are kept on small farms to be butchered for food. Nomadic herders roam the savanna in search of grazing land for their herds. Immigrants from drought-stricken Chad and Sudan have brought many cattle into the country. In many cases, hunting is more important than herding. Much of the country's meat supply comes from wild game. Only occasionally will an average family serve a domestic chicken or goat at a family meal, since these animals may represent a big portion of their wealth. For people living near the nation's many rivers, fish can be a big source of protein. Some fish farms raise fish such as tilapia in ponds.

Forestry is a major business in the southwest, especially along the borders with Cameroon and the Republic of the Congo. Timber production has more than doubled since the early 1990s, and timber has become one of the nation's most profitable exports. However, logging companies do not replace the trees that they cut down, leading to a reduced area suitable for logging. The majority of the nation's timber is obeche, sapele, ebony, and sipo.

A girl leads her family's cattle. Animals such as cattle and chickens are the most valuable thing many families in the CAR own.

Services

Services provide about 25 percent of the GDP in the CAR. Service businesses include banking, real estate, retail sales, transportation, and tourism. Civil servants, such as police, teachers, and other government workers, are also part of the services sector. The government's inability to pay civil servants has been a major problem for the CAR for decades, however. Teachers and other civil servants have held strike after strike over the decades, but the government treasury usually remains bare.

Street vendors are the dominant sales force in the country. The nation has few modern shops, and those it has are all in Bangui. Street vendors—mostly women—sell food, clothing, tools, crafts, religious objects, and much more.

In the past, tourism was a major part of the Central African economy. But political instability in recent years has greatly reduced the number of tourists visiting the country. Those tourists who do visit come to see the nation's wide variety

BARGAINING POWER

Bargaining is an expected part of buying or selling anything in the CAR. The process begins with the seller offering a price. The buyer then counters with a lower price. The two parties exchange offers until they agree on a price. But there are unwritten rules about how to counter. For example, textiles are one product where there is little room for negotiation. If a buyer suggests a price that is much too low, it is an insult to the seller. The seller may refuse to deal further with the buyer, even if the buyer's offer increases.

Women sell food at a market.

of wildlife in the nation's parks and reserves. Others come to hunt or fish for trophies. Waterfalls near Boali and the Bouar megaliths are other popular tourist attractions.

Industry and Mining

Together, industry and mining account for 20 percent of the nation's GDP. The CAR has few traditional factories, focusing instead on producing raw materials such as timber, diamonds, gold, and uranium. What little manufacturing exists in the country is centered almost entirely in Bangui. It includes furniture workshops, soap factories, food processing plants, and textile mills. The CAR has several small plants that extract oils from sesame seeds, peanuts, and palm nuts. Ginneries, which separate raw cotton from its seeds, are well established in Berbérati and other regional towns. Other finished products produced in the CAR include shoes, motorcycles, and bicycles. Sawmills produce lumber, while breweries produce beer.

Mining is by far the largest part of the industry sector. Most mining activity in the CAR centers on its diamond deposits, which are located in the western part of the country. The country produces more than five hundred thousand carats of diamonds per year (a carat is equal to 0.2 grams, or 0.007 ounce), and that figure may be low because of rampant illegal diamond smuggling. About 75 percent of the diamonds produced in the CAR are of gem quality, meaning they're suitable for jewelry. The remaining 25 percent are used for industrial uses (as

Villagers dig for diamonds in a mine in the northeastern CAR.

CHILDREN OF THE STREET

The streets of Bangui are filled with groups of children called *godobe*. These children, who either have no families or have left home because their families could not provide for them, must fend for themselves on the harsh streets of the city. They form their own social structure, gathering in groups for protection.

The godobe do whatever they can to survive. Many seek out odd jobs. They might deliver packages, watch over parked cars, or deliver water to street vendors. Others turn to begging, theft, or prostitution. Drug use is high among the godobe, making their difficult existence bleaker still.

abrasives or on cutting tools). The money generated from the diamond industry does little to help the people of the CAR, however. Most of it funnels through foreign companies and a select few Central Africans.

The diamond industry uses an open-pit technique, in which miners remove dirt and rock from the surface of a strip of land as they search for diamonds. Miners often work in small groups during the dry season and return each year to their previously established pits. Smaller mining operations take place on the rivers. Production and export levels rise and fall, depending upon the agreements between the government and foreign diamond companies, which regulate the market. Most diamonds are exported in raw, uncut form. A government organization in Bangui maintains a local cutting operation.

Other mineral resources in the nation include gold, uranium, and iron. But the CAR lacks the resources and infrastructure to exploit these minerals. Gold production was once high but has fallen off vastly in recent decades. Uranium was discovered in 1966, but the high start-up cost of mining it and transporting it has left the resource largely untapped. Some geologists have suggested that the CAR probably has oil deposits as well, but little effort has been made to search for them.

Foreign Trade

The CAR, with its political instability and undeveloped infrastructure, attracts little foreign investment. Exports include timber, cotton, coffee, and tobacco. Diamonds, however, make up the largest share of the nation's exports. Most raw diamonds are shipped to Belgium for cutting, though Spain, France, Italy, and a few other countries also get some Central African diamonds. Other trading partners include Cameroon and DRC, as well as the United States, China, and Japan.

Central African imports include food, fuel, industrial supplies and machinery, automobiles, and consumer goods. Because of the nation's inability to produce finished goods, in addition to its lack of exports, the CAR generally runs a trade deficit (meaning it imports more goods than it exports).

Transportation and Communication

With its lack of a seaport and railroads, as well as its largely undeveloped infrastructure, moving people and goods around in the CAR can be a challenge. The nation has about 14,800 miles (23,818 km) of roads, but less than 400 miles (644 km) of that is paved. Many of the roads, especially in remote areas, are little more than worn dirt paths that get little to no maintenance. The nation has few cars, and most of what it has are in Bangui. Taxi and bus services are available in Bangui as well. People traveling from town to town may walk or ride bikes.

Many foreigners are surprised by how people in the Central African Republic drive. Drivers tend to ignore traffic laws. For example, they drive on whatever part of the road is in the best shape—even if that's right down the middle!

Travelers walk down a highway in the Central African Republic. Very few people in the CAR own a vehicle.

Because of the lack of good roads or a railroad service, rivers are a main source of transportation in the CAR. Many people use small canoes called pirogues to get around. These small, lightweight canoes are basically hollowed out tree trunks. They can be paddled or punted (pushed) with a long pole.

The CAR has more than fifty airports, but only three of them have paved runways. Five airlines—most notably Air Afrique—provide flights at the nation's international airport in Bangui. Within the country, Inter-RCA is the main carrier.

The nation's waterways are a major source of transport. Of the CAR's roughly 4,400 miles (7,081 km) of waterways, about 40 percent are navigable. Barges carry goods up and down the Oubangui and other rivers. Exports are shipped from the Oubangui to the Congo River and from there to the Republic of the Congo's Atlantic port of Pointe-Noire.

People often use **boats to travel** in the CAR. This group is crossing a river.

Communications systems are also mostly undeveloped. Electrical service is rare, especially in rural areas. So the nation has few televisions and other modern conveniences. Telephones are both scarce and expensive, and the nation never really built an adequate system for landlines. Those who do have personal phones usually have cell phones.

Likewise, computers are rare in the CAR. An estimated five thousand Central Africans access the Internet regularly. Many of those do so in Internet cafés in Bangui.

With few homes getting electrical service, the CAR's power needs are modest. About 80 percent of the nation's electricity comes from hydroelectric dams on its many rivers.

◎ The Future

With a struggling economy, undeveloped infrastructure, and rampant political corruption, the CAR faces a host of daunting challenges as it looks toward the future. For centuries its people have been isolated from the world—and more important, from one another. To move forward into a modern, global economy, the nation's people will have to come together to form a true sense of national unity.

Despite all the hurdles, there are reasons for hope. The CAR has a wealth of natural resources, from fertile farmland to diamonds to raw natural beauty. If it can achieve political stability, tourism could prove a critical element toward repairing the economy. The CAR's people are as varied as its landscape. If they can find common ground and common purpose, they can begin to build a brighter, more prosperous future for themselves and for future generations.

Visit www.vgsbooks.com for links to websites with news on the economic situation in the Central African Republic.

6000 B.C.	Groups of nomadic hunter-gatherers live in the region, moving in search of food and prey.
500 B.C.	An unknown civilization erects a set of megaliths used for astronomical observation.
A.D. 1000	Several groups live in the area, using slash-and-burn methods to clear land for farming.
1600s	Arab traders come to the area, seizing local peoples and selling them in the slave trade. This practice continues for more than two hundred years.
CA. 1820	The Baya-Mandija people migrate into the present-day CAR as they flee slave raiders to the north.
CA. 1850	The Bobangi people raid the nearby Gbaya and Mandija peoples, capturing slaves to sell and instilling deep resentments between the groups.
1880s	France annexes (takes control of) the area.
1889	France establishes the city of Bangui.
1903	France officially names the territory Oubangui-Chari, with Bangui as its capital.
1906–1909	Baram-Bakie leads the Vridi people in a revolt against the French colonists.
1910	France establishes French Equatorial Africa (AEF), which includes Oubangui-Chari, Gabon, Congo, and Chad.
1914	Diamonds are discovered near the town of Ippy.
1920s	The French government forces thousands of men from Oubangui-Chari to work on the Congo-Ocean Railroad, hundreds of miles from their homes. Central Africans stage violent protests against forced labor and other injustices.
1938	A crop disease destroys many of the coffee trees in the region.
1939–1945	World War II rages in Europe, Asia, and North Africa. Soldiers from Oubangui-Chari fight in support of the French. Members of the region's different ethnic groups fight side by side and develop a national identity that results in an independence movement.
1946	French president Charles de Gaulle organizes French holdings into the French Union. Barthélemy Boganda becomes the first Central African elected to the French National Assembly.
1957	Boganda and his party, the Movement for the Social Evolution of Black Africa (MESAN), score overwhelming victories in the territorial assembly election. Boganda becomes president of the assembly.
1958	The French dissolve French Equatorial Africa. Oubangui-Chari is renamed the Central African Republic, an autonomous territory.

1959 On March 29, Boganda is killed in a plane crash. Many Central Africans find the circumstances of his death suspicious.

1960 On August 13, the CAR achieves full independence from France. David Dacko is elected by the National Assembly as the new nation's first president.

1962 Dacko makes MESAN the nation's only legal political party.

1965 Sango joins French as a national language of the CAR. On December 31, Jean-Bedel Bokassa leads a nearly bloodless coup, taking over control of the CAR and dissolving the National Assembly.

1972 Pierre Makombo Bamboté publishes his acclaimed novel *Princesse Mandapu*.

1975 Bokassa appoints Elisabeth Domitien as the nation's prime minister, making her the first female prime minister of an African nation.

1976 Bokassa renames the CAR the Central African Empire and declares himself emperor.

1979 Angered by the protests of students, Bokassa sets off the bloody Children's Massacre at Bangui. A panel of judges charges Bokassa with murder. The French react quickly, supporting a coup led by Dacko, who is restored to the office of president. The country's name reverts to the Central African Republic.

1981 General André Kolingba leads a coup that removes the unpopular Dacko from office.

1986 Under international pressure, Kolingba reforms the National Assembly.

1991 The National Assembly revises the CAR's constitution to allow for a multiparty legislature. Singer Princess Leoni Kangala releases her first solo album, *Sengue Sengue*.

1993 Ange-Felix Patassé beats Kolingba and Dacko in elections to become president and end twelve years of military rule.

1996 Angry over unpaid wages, soldiers loot and riot in Bangui.

1999 Patassé is reelected president with an overwhelming majority of the votes.

2003 With the help of Libyan troops, François Bozizé ousts Patassé and takes control of the CAR.

2005 Bozizé is elected president. Flooding in Bangui leaves twenty thousand people homeless.

2006 Rebels seize the northeastern town of Birao.

2007 French jets bomb Birao, putting down the rebel surge and also leaving thousands of Central Africans homeless.

2008 Teachers and civil servants in the CAR strike to protest months of nonpayment of wages. The strike leads to the resignation of Prime Minister Elie Dote. Bozizé names Faustin Archange Touadera the new prime minister.

COUNTRY NAME Central African Republic

AREA 240,535 square miles (622,984 sq. km)

MAIN LANDFORMS Plateau, Yadé Massif, Bongo Massif, Tondou Massif, Karre Mountains, Rain Forest

HIGHEST POINT Mount Ngaoui, 4,658 feet (1,420 meters)

LOWEST POINT Oubangui River, 1,099 feet (335 m)

MAJOR RIVERS Oubangui, Chari, Sangha

ANIMALS antelope, bongos, buffalo, cheetahs, chimpanzees, giraffes, gorillas, hippos, leopards, lions, monkeys, rhinos, tsetse flies, zebras

CAPITAL CITY Bangui

OTHER MAJOR CITIES Bimbo, Berbérati, Carnot, Bambari, Bouar, Bossangoa

OFFICIAL LANGUAGES French and Sango

MONETARY UNIT CFA franc (1 CFA franc = 100 centimes)

CAR CURRENCY

The official currency of the CAR is the CFA franc. CFA stands for Communauté Financière Africaine, or African Financial Community. The CFA franc is also the currency in the neighboring countries of Cameroon, Chad, Republic of the Congo, Equatorial Guinea, and Gabon. The franc is divided into 100 centimes. Banknotes are printed in denominations of 500, 1,000, 2,000, 5,000, and 10,000, while coins are made in denominations of 1, 2, 5, 10, 25, 50, 100, 500 francs (no coins or notes are broken down into centimes). One U.S. dollar is worth about 440 CFA francs, though that ratio varies widely.

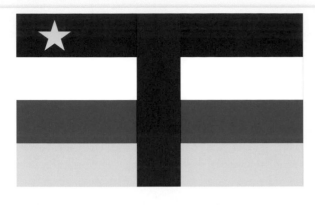

The flag of the CAR was adopted on December 1, 1958. Barthélemy Boganda, the nation's first prime minister, originally designed it for the United States of Latin Africa. But when the unification of the states failed to happen, he used it for the CAR instead. Boganda combined the red, white, and blue of the French flag with green and yellow, colors that represent Africa. Four horizontal stripes are cut in half by a vertical red stripe. A yellow star lies in the flag's upper left corner. The red stripe symbolizes the blood spilled to gain independence. The blue represents the sky and freedom. The white stands for peace, while the green represents hope, and yellow stands for tolerance.

Barthélemy Boganda wrote the lyrics for the CAR's national anthem, "La Renaissance" (also called "E Zingo" in Sango). The anthem was adopted in 1960. Herbert Pepper composed the music. The anthem is usually sung in French. Here are the lyrics translated into English:

La Renaissance
Oh! Central Africa, cradle of the Bantu!
Take up again your right to respect, to life!
Long subjugated, long scorned by all,
But, from today, breaking tyranny's hold.
Through work, order and dignity
You reconquer your rights, your unity,
And to take this new step
The voice of our ancestors call us.

CHORUS:
To work! In order and dignity,
in the respect for rights and in unity,
Breaking poverty and tyranny,
Holding high the flag of the Fatherland.

For a link to a site where you can listen to the Central African Republic's national anthem, visit www.vgsbooks.com.

BARTHÉLEMY BOGANDA (1910–1959) A national hero in the CAR, Boganda was born in the village of Bobangui in the far southwestern part of the country. He was adopted and raised by Catholic missionaries and in 1938 was ordained as a priest. In 1946 he became the first resident of the Oubangui-Chari territory to be elected to the French National Assembly. He formed Movement for the Social Evolution of Black Africa (MESAN) and fought for the rights of the working class. Boganda became the territory's first prime minister and was set to become the nation's first president—he even designed the nation's flag and wrote its national anthem. However, he was killed under mysterious circumstances in a 1959 plane crash. His legacy lives on, however, and he is considered the father of the CAR.

FRANÇOIS BOZIZÉ (b. 1946) The president of the CAR was born in the nation of Gabon. As a teen, Bozizé went to a military training school in Bouar. He quickly worked his way up the ranks of the CAR military and was appointed brigadier general by Bokassa in 1978. After surviving the turmoil of the 1980s and early 1990s (including time in exile and time under arrest for his politics), Bozizé rose back to the top of the CAR military alongside Ange-Felix Patassé, whom he had supported for years. Patassé named him chief of staff of the armed forces but dismissed him in 2001 with questions about his loyalty. Two years later, with the help of forces from Chad, Bozizé overthrew Patassé and took control for himself. He was formally elected president in 2005.

ELISABETH DOMITIEN (1925–2005) Born in the southwestern part of the Central African Republic, Domitien became interested in politics at an early age and became a member of the MESAN. She rose through the party's ranks and supported Bokassa's coup in 1965. With Bokassa in power, she grew more and more powerful, becoming MESAN's vice president in 1972. In 1975 Bokassa appointed her to the newly created position of prime minister (making her the first female prime minister of an African nation). But in 1976, when she opposed his proposal for a monarchy, Bokassa dismissed her from the position. She was arrested and served a prison term in 1979, after Bokassa was overthrown. She never returned to politics but remained a prominent businesswoman in the CAR until her death in 2005.

PRINCESS LEONI KANGALA (b. 1953) The daughter of a politician, Kangala was born in Bossangoa. Her father was a close associate of Boganda and was killed with the leader in 1959. After finishing her education, Kangala took a job as a broadcaster with the state-run TV station, TVCA. After two years on the air, she moved on to various government jobs. In 1977 she and her brothers formed a musical group, Manganga. Soon after, she moved to France to pursue a music career. She released her first solo album in 1991 and another in 1996. Her music combines traditional Central African sounds with soul, funk, dance, and other styles.

ANGE-FELIX PATASSÉ (b. 1937) The former president was born in the northwestern town of Paoua. He studied zoo technology in Paris before returning to the CAR in 1959. He worked in the nation's Ministry of Agriculture, and in 1965, Dacko named him director of agriculture and minister of development. He became a trusted ally of Bokassa after the 1966 coup and held a variety of government positions, including prime minister from 1976 to 1978. He came in second to Dacko in a 1981 election, though many believe the election was rigged. He ran again and won in 1993. He is widely regarded as the nation's first fairly elected president. He was reelected in 1999, despite the nation's dire economic problems. In 2003, while in a conference abroad, Bozizé led a coup and took control of the country. Patassé wanted to run in the 2005 presidential election but was banned by Bozizé under allegations he had stolen from the country's treasury.

JÉRÔME RAMEDANE (1936–1991) Born in the present-day town of Kaga-Bandoro, the CAR's most famous painter was a man of small stature. He was teased relentlessly for his small size and so retreated into the world of art for escape. At first, lacking canvases, he painted the outsides of houses. He depicted scenes of rural life, history, hunting, and farming. As his fame grew, he moved on to oil paints and canvas. Among his most famous works is *Animals in the Forest*, which depicts a lion lying in the grass, with a water buffalo and two antelope in the background.

PIERRE SAMMY MACKFOY (b. 1935) One of the CAR's best-known authors, Mackfoy was born in Bangassou, in the eastern part of the country. He studied in Europe, earning an undergraduate degree in the arts and a postgraduate degree in education. He began his popular Mongou stories in 1967 with the publication of *Mongou, Son of Bandia*. Mackfoy has also written nonfiction, as well as numerous textbooks for Central African schools. He has served as the CAR's minister of national education as well as in the National Assembly. He also cofounded the Central African Writers' Association.

SISTER ZOUNGOULA (CA. 1880–1909) Sister Zoungoula was born into slavery. Little is known of her early life. But in 1892, Catholic missionary Monsignor Prosper Augouard brought her and another former slave named Kalouka to the Catholic mission in Brazzaville (in neighboring Congo). There, the former slaves were educated before joining the Holy Ghost Order as nuns. The two devoted their lives to the care of leprosy victims in the region—including parts of the present-day CAR. Both women eventually contracted and died from the disease. Their names have since surfaced as candidates for Catholic sainthood.

Sights to See

The Central African Republic is a land of great natural beauty. But its unstable political situation makes it a dangerous place. People considering a visit should first check with the U.S. State Department (see website at http://travel.state.gov/travel/warnings.html) to determine the safety of visiting the region.

BANGUI The only big city in the CAR is the center of Central African culture. The Boganda Museum offers a peek into the region's history, while those seeking a taste of modern culture can visit the shops, restaurants, and dance clubs of the famous K-Cinq intersection. The Avenue Boganda is the city's main commercial district and is scattered with shops.

BOALI WATERFALLS The waterfalls on the Mbali River (a tributary of the Oubangui River) near the small town of Boali are one of the most beautiful spots in the CAR. Visitors can also tour the large hydroelectric dam that controls the flow to the falls.

BOUAR MEGALITHS Ancient stone megaliths stand outside the town of Bouar in the western part of the country. Much like the more famous megaliths at Stonehenge in Great Britain, these stones helped ancient people track the movements of the stars and planets.

DZANGA-SANGHA RESERVE For those wanting to see the wildlife of the CAR, Dzanga-Sangha Reserve is a perfect spot. Visitors can see gorillas, elephants, and much more.

KEMBE FALLS The falls on the Kotto River (a tributary of the Oubangui) near Bangassou isn't a developed tourist area, but the impressive whitewater falls still draw many visitors to the area.

MANOVO-GOUNDA SAINT FLORIS NATIONAL PARK A United Nations Educational, Scientific, and Cultural Organization (UNESCO) World Heritage Site, this park is near the Chad border. Visitors can see black rhinos, elephants, cheetahs, leopards, gazelles, African buffalo, and more.

MBAÏKI This town is surrounded by forest and is home to many of the pygmy people. Tourists can buy carefully carved pieces of ebony and enjoy nearby waterfalls.

ZINGA This small river town features wooden houses (a rarity in the CAR) and is a hub for boat traffic on the Oubangui River.

animism: a belief system based on the idea that all things—animate and inanimate—have spirits or souls

coup: the forceful and quick overthrow of government by a small group

desertification: a process in which fertile land becomes very dry or desert-like. The CAR and other nations in the Sahel region struggle with desertification as the Sahara expands southward.

godobe: groups of homeless children living on the streets of Bangui

gross domestic product (GDP): a measure of the total value of goods and services produced within the boundaries of a country in a certain amount of time (usually one year)

Harmattan: a dry and dusty wind that blows south off the Sahara from about November to March

infrastructure: the system of public works, such as roads, power lines, and telephone lines, of a country

kodros: residential neighborhoods in Bangui, usually with buildings made from mud bricks and thatched roofs

massif: a compact group of mountains, especially one that is not connected to other chains or groups of mountains

megalith: a large stone monument. The megaliths near Bouar helped ancient peoples track the movements of the stars and planets.

orature: oral history and folktales that are told rather than written down

pirogue: a canoe made from a hollowed-out log

pygmy: a broad term used to describe the Aka, Baka, and Twa peoples, known for their small stature

Sahel: a climatic zone in Africa. Not as dry as the Sahara, the Sahel makes up a large region to the south of the Sahara.

syncreticism: the combination of different religious beliefs, such as the blending of Christianity with indigenous beliefs such as ancestor worship and animism

Central Intelligence Agency (CIA). *The World Factbook: Central African Republic. 2008.*
https://www.cia.gov/library/publications/the-world-factbook/geos/ct.html (April 1, 2008).
This source offers statistics and background information on the Central African Republic's economy, history, demographics, and more.

Dalby, Andrew. *Dictionary of Languages: The Definitive Reference to More Than 400 Languages.* **New York: Columbia University Press, 2004.**
Dalby explores the origins, history, and uses of more than four hundred languages, including Sango and several other Central African tongues.

Europa World Yearbook, 2007. **Vol. I. London: Europa Publications, 2007.**
Covering the Central African Republic's recent history, economy, and government, this annual publication also provides a wealth of statistics on population, employment, trade, and more.

Kalck, Pierre. *Historical Dictionary of the Central African Republic.* **3rd ed. Translated by Thomas O'Toole. Metuchen, NJ: Scarecrow Press, 2004.**
The people, places, and major events of the history of the CAR are listed alphabetically and briefly described in this resource. A timeline and a lengthy list of sources are also provided.

O'Toole, Thomas. "The Central African Republic: Political Reform and Social Malaise." **In John F. Clark and David E. Gardinier, eds.,** *Political Reform in Francophone Africa.* **Boulder, CO: Westview Press, 1997.**
O'Toole explores attempts at political reform in the CAR during the late 1990s, just after the height of the army mutiny crisis in Bangui.

———. *The Central African Republic: The Continent's Hidden Heart.* **Boulder, CO: Westview Press, 1986.**
This title in the Nations of Contemporary Africa series provides a detailed history of the Central African Republic and its people through the mid-1980s.

PRB. "PRB 2007 World Population Data Sheet." *Population Reference Bureau (PRB).*
2007. http://www.prb.org (April 1, 2008).
This annual statistics sheet provides a wealth of data on the Central African Republic's population, birthrates and death rates, fertility rate, infant mortality rate, and other useful demographic information.

Smith, Alex Duval. "France Admits Air Raids on Darfur Neighbours." *Independent.* **December 15, 2006.**
http://www.independent.co.uk/news/world/africa/france-admits-air-raids-on-darfur-neighbours-428546.html (April 1, 2008).
This story covers France's 2006 admission of its military actions in Sudan's Darfur region and nearby areas—including the Central African Republic.

U.S. Department of State: Bureau of African Affairs. "Central African Republic." *Background Notes*. 2008.
http://www.state.gov/r/pa/ei/bgn/4007.htm (April 1, 2008).
This overview, published annually and regularly updated by the U.S. government, provides an introduction to the Central African Republic's government, history, foreign relations, and more.

Woodfork, Jacqueline Cassandra. *Culture and Customs of the Central African Republic*. Westport, CT: Greenwood Press, 2006.
This in-depth look at the culture and people of the Central African Republic covers subjects ranging from religion and worldview to music, literature, and the arts.

Woodfork, Jacqueline C., and Joel Charny. "The Central African Republic: Worsening Crisis in a Troubled Region." *United States Institute of Peace*. September 2007.
http://www.usip.org/pubs/usipeace_briefings/2007/0911_central_african_republic.html (April 1, 2008).
The authors explain the historical background for the current unrest in the Central African Republic and examine the rebels who are fighting against the nation's government.

Africa: Explore the Regions: Sahel
http://www.pbs.org/wnet/africa/explore/sahel/sahel_overview_lo.html
This PBS website introduces visitors to the people, geography, and environment of the Sahel region of Africa.

AllAfrica.com—Central African Republic
http://allafrica.com/centralafricanrepublic
Keep up with the latest news from the Central African Republic at this site, which gathers news items from a variety of sources.

BBC News, Country Profile: Central African Republic
http://news.bbc.co.uk/2/hi/africa/country_profiles/1067518.stm
The BBC's country profile of the Central African Republic gives an overview of the nation, some fast facts, information about current leaders, and news updates.

Bowden, Rob. *Africa South of the Sahara.* **Chicago: Heinemann Library, 2008.**
Learn about the central and southern parts of Africa, their people, geography, resources, and more.

Cordell, Dennis D. *Dar al-Kuti and the Last Years of the Trans-Saharan Slave Trade.* **Madison: University of Wisconsin Press, 1985.**
Cordell examines the Arab role and impact on the slave trade in central Africa, especially in the region of present-day Chad and Central African Republic.

DiPiazza, Francesca. *Sudan in Pictures.* **Minneapolis: Twenty-First Century Books, 2006.**
Read about the land, history, people, economy, and culture of Sudan, the Central African Republic's eastern neighbor.

Dzanga-Sangha: The Rainforest Reserve in CAR
http://www.dzanga-sangha.org/en/index.php
Learn all about the plants, animals, and other attractions of the Dzanga-Sangha Reserve. The site has a wealth of photographs of gorillas, elephants, and other animals. You can also read about the pygmies who call the forest home.

"Inside France's Secret War."
http://www.independent.co.uk/news/world/africa/inside-frances-secret-war-396062.html
The writer tells the story of more than forty years of French military actions in and around the Central African Republic, culminating with gripping firsthand accounts of the 2007 bombing of the town of Birao.

Lyman, Francesca. *Inside the Dzanga Sangha Rain Forest: Exploring the Heart of Central Africa.* **New York: Workman Publishing, 1998.**
This resource follows a group of scientists, artists, and filmmakers as they search the Central African rain forest for gorillas, rare birds, leopards, elephants, and more.

Further Reading and Websites

Portals to the World—Central African Republic
http://www.loc.gov/rr/international/amed/centralafricanrepublic/
centralafricanrepublic.html
The Library of Congress's list of selected websites on the CAR covers a broad range of categories, including government, media and communication, recreation and travel, and religion and philosophy.

Silver, Donald M. *African Savanna*. New York: Learning Triangle Press, 1997.
Read about the grasslands that stretch across Africa south of the Sahara and discover the animals that live there.

Stevens, Stuart. *Malaria Dreams: An African Adventure*. New York: Atlantic Monthly Press, 1994.
In a fascinating account, Stevens tells of a driving trip he took across the CAR, Cameroon, Chad, Niger, Mali, and Algeria.

Strong, Polly, trans. *African Tales: Folklore of the Central African Republic*. Mogadore, OH: Telcraft, 1992.
The fascinating stories and folktales of Central African people, including the Mandjia and the Banda, are translated into English in this book.

Titley, Brian. *Dark Age: The Political Odyssey of Emperor Bokassa*. London: McGill-Queen's University Press, 1997.
The author examines the rise to power and administration of one of the CAR's most influencial and controversial leaders, self-proclaimed Emperor Jean-Bedel Bokassa.

vgsbooks.com
http://www.vgsbooks.com
Visit vgsbooks.com, the home page of the Visual Geography Series®. You can get linked to all sorts of useful online information, including geographical, historical, demographic, cultural, and economic websites. The vgsbooks.com site is a great resource for late-breaking news and statistics.

Zuchora-Walske, Christine. *Chad in Pictures*. Minneapolis: Twenty-First Century Books, 2009.
The Central African Republic shares more with its northern neighbor than just a border. Learn about the geography, people, and culture of Chad.

Captions for photos appearing on cover and chapter openers:

Cover: A fisherman casts a net into the Dzanga River in southwestern Central African Republic.

pp. 4–5 A fishing village stands on the edge of the Oubangui River.

pp. 8–9 A lush savanna grows at the heart of the Central African Republic.

pp. 36–37 A group of boys pose for a picture after swimming in a river in southwestern CAR.

pp. 46–47 Children in a Bayanga village in southwestern Central African Republic perform for a traditional festival.

pp. 56–57 Buyers and sellers mingle at a busy market in a village near Bangassou.

Photo Acknowledgments

The images in this book are used with the permission of: © Victor Englebert, pp. 4–5, 8–9, 11, 15, 50; © XNR Productions, pp. 6, 10; © Dr. John Michael Fay/ National Geographic /Getty Images, pp. 13, 14; ©Juan Vrijdag/drr.net, pp. 17, 36–37, 48, 64; © akg-images/Coll.Archiv f.Kunst & Geschichte, p. 21; © Albert Harlingue/Roger Violet/The Image Works, p. 22; © Roger-Viollet/The Image Works, p. 25; © AFP/Getty Images, p. 26; © Kean Collection/Getty Images, p. 27; © Pierre Gillaud/AFP/Getty Images, p. 28; © JEAN-CLAUDE DELMAS/ AFP/Getty Images, p. 30; © CHRISTOPHE SIMON/AFP/Getty Images, p. 31; © DESIRAY MINKOH/AFP/Getty Images, pp. 32, 33, 51; AP Photo/Schalk van Zuydam, p. 34; © Giacamo Pirozzi/Panos Pictures, pp. 39, 45, 54, 60; © Juan Vrijdan/Panos Pictures, p. 40; © Ton Koene/Peter Arnold, Inc., p. 41; © Spencer Platt/Getty Images, pp. 42 (both), 59; © LIONEL HEALING/AFP/ Getty Images, p. 44; © Ivan Vdovin/Alamy, pp. 46–47; REUTERS/David Lewis, pp. 53, 61; © Mary Jelliffe/Art Directors & TRIP, pp. 56–57; © Warren Jacobs/ Art Directors & TRIP, p. 58; © Sylvia Cordaiy Photo Library Ltd./Alamy, p. 63; Audrius Tomonis—www.banknotes.com, p. 68; © Laura Westlund/ Independent Picture Service, p. 69.

Front Cover: © Martin Harvey/Alamy.